BRIGHT IDEA BOOKS

BIGFOOT

by Bradley Cole

CAPSTONE PRESS
a capstone imprint

Bright Idea Books are published by Capstone Press
1710 Roe Crest Drive, North Mankato, Minnesota 56003
www.mycapstone.com

Library of Congress Cataloging-in-Publication Data
Names: Cole, Bradley, author.
Title: Bigfoot / by Bradley Cole.
Description: North Mankato, MN : Capstone Press, 2020. | Series: Monster histories | Includes index. | Audience: Grade 4 to 6. |
Identifiers: LCCN 2019003133 (print) | LCCN 2019005912 (ebook) | ISBN 9781543571301 (ebook) | ISBN 9781543571219 (hardcover) | ISBN 9781543574982 (paperback)
Subjects: LCSH: Sasquatch--Juvenile literature.
Classification: LCC QL89.2.S2 (ebook) | LCC QL89.2.S2 C645 2020 (print) | DDC 001.944--dc23
LC record available at https://lccn.loc.gov/2019003133

All internet sites appearing in back matter were available and accurate when this book was sent to press.

Editorial Credits
Editor: Claire Vanden Branden
Designer: Becky Daum
Production Specialist: Colleen McLaren

Photo Credits
Alamy: Sputnik, 10; iStockphoto: BarashenkovAnton, 14–15, Big_Ryan, cover (Bigfoot), KLH49, 16–17, PeopleImages, 31, Rich Legg, 26–27, RichVintage, 5; Shutterstock Images: Erik Mandre, 19, Kyrylo Glivin, 20–21, matej spiroch, 22, Oleg Moskaliuk, 6–7, Paul Juser, 8–9, Robsonphoto, cover (background), Rudy Riva, 13, 28, Vjaceslav K, 25

Design Elements: Shutterstock Images, Red Line Editorial

Printed and bound in the USA. PO5819

TABLE OF CONTENTS

CHAPTER 1

WHAT IS Bigfoot?

There is something in the woods. Hikers find huge footprints. A shadow moves ahead. The hikers quickly snap a photo. The picture is only a **blur** behind a tree. Could it be Bigfoot?

Bigfoot is also known as Sasquatch.

Bigfoot is a hairy creature. Some people think it is real. They say it looks like an ape. It also looks like a bear. Bigfoot walks on two legs. It is between 6 feet (1.8 meters) and 15 feet (4.6 m) tall. Most tales say it is from the northwestern United States. Some say it is from western Canada.

People think Bigfoot can be found in wooded areas.

FOOTPRINT SIGHTING

Bigfoot stories have been around for many years. David Thompson was an explorer. He said he found strange footprints in 1811. This was one of the first recorded sightings of a footprint. Many people have reported seeing Bigfoot since then.

Some people think this is what a Bigfoot footprint looks like.

Many Bigfoot believers around the world use Roger Patterson's and Bob Gimlin's video as proof that Bigfoot is real.

The most famous Bigfoot sighting was in 1967. Two men were in Bluff Creek, California. Their names were Roger Patterson and Bob Gimlin. They went out looking for Bigfoot. They made a short video of what they saw. In it a large creature walks through the forest. It is hard to tell what it is. Many people think it is Bigfoot. Others think it is just a person in a costume. No one knows for sure.

CHAPTER 2

INTEREST Grows

Bigfoot became known around the world. Every year thousands of people say they see it. Some people try to hunt Bigfoot. They look for clues in the forest.

BIGFOOT BELIEVERS

In the United States, 29 percent of people believe Bigfoot is real. In Canada, that number is at 21 percent.

Some signs have been put up in areas where people said they saw Bigfoot.

PHOTOS AND FAKES

People say they have taken pictures of Bigfoot. The photos are blurry. It is hard to tell if the object is real or not.

People also say they have found **evidence** of Bigfoot. Many people search in large groups. They take pictures of animal **tracks**. But many pictures turn out to be fake. Sometimes the tracks are real. But they are often from a bear.

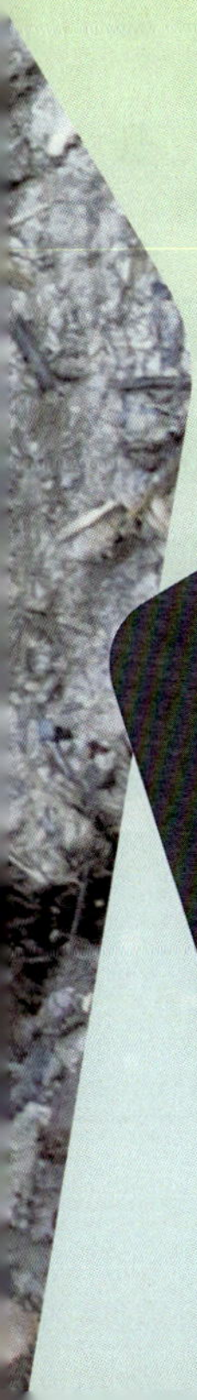

Sometimes people think bear footprints are Bigfoot footprints.

People have also found hair in the woods. They bring it to get tested. But it is just elk or bear fur.

Sometimes people dress up as Bigfoot. They want others to say they saw the creature. This makes photos of Bigfoot hard to believe. It could just be a person in a costume.

Sometimes people dress up in Bigfoot costumes to fool others into thinking Bigfoot is real.

CHAPTER 3

RECENT Sightings

Rick Jacobs thought he got photos of Bigfoot in 2007. His camera took the photos at night. They show an animal by a tree. But it might have just been a sick bear.

Bears are often mistaken for Bigfoot.

In 2012 Rick Dyer said he shot Bigfoot in Texas. He said he had Bigfoot's body. He got it tested. The **DNA** test came back as unknown. But he would not show the test results or body to anyone.

When scientists test the DNA in blood, they can tell what kind of animal it came from.

Dyer later said his story was a lie. The Bigfoot body was fake. It was made out of rubber and hair.

Gorillas can look similar to Bigfoot when they are walking on their back legs.

A man in Mississippi took a video in 2013. He thinks it is of Bigfoot. He was hunting when he saw it. The creature in the video looked like a bear. It also looked like a gorilla. No one knows for sure what it was.

YETI

There are tales of a hairy monster in Asia too. It is called a yeti.

CHAPTER 4

IS BIGFOOT Real?

Some say more people would have seen Bigfoot if it were real. There would be many Bigfoots in the world. Scientists say there should be old Bigfoot bodies. People would find old Bigfoot bones.

Animal bones can be found in the wild. Scientists say we would find Bigfoot bones if the creature existed.

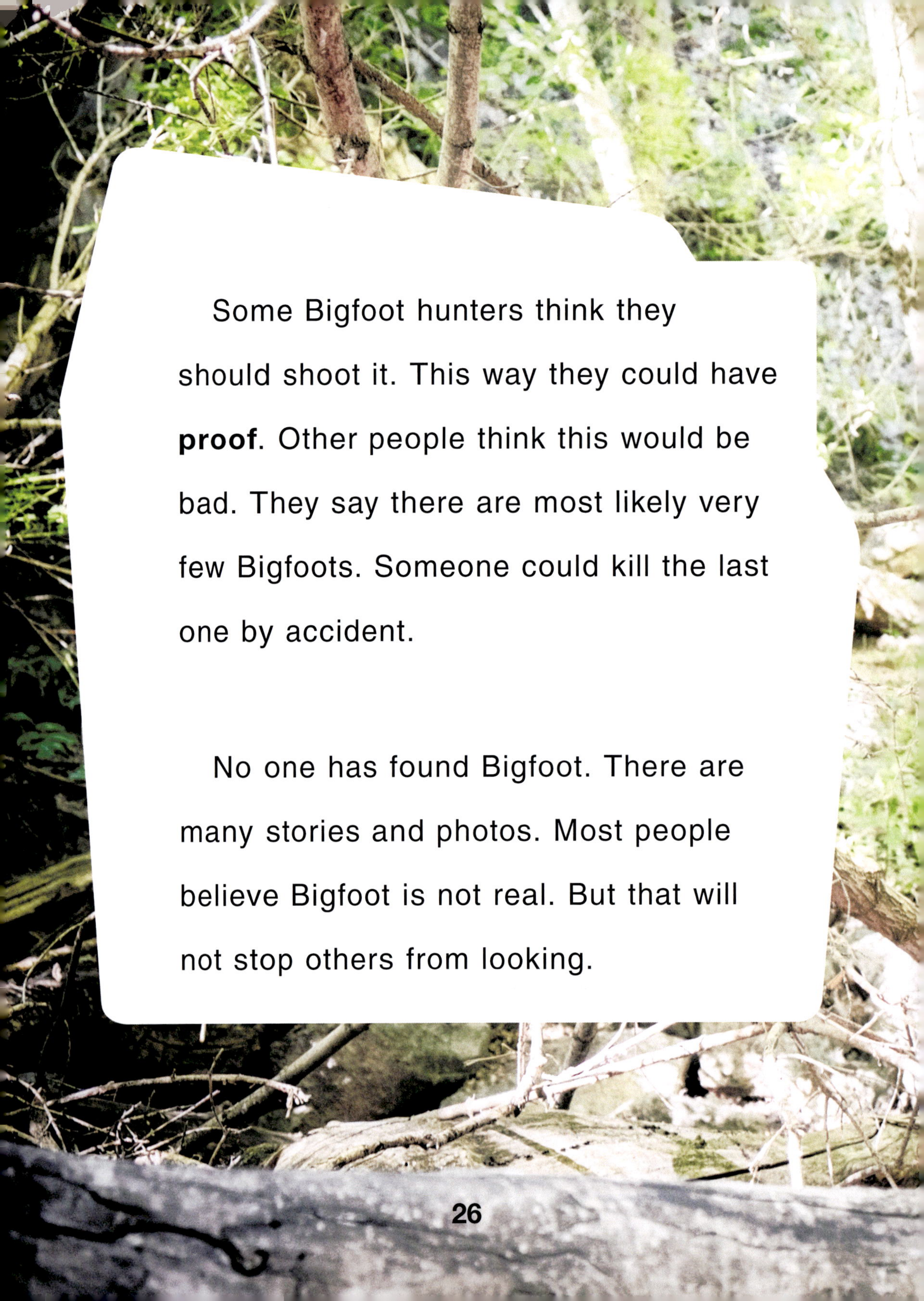

Some Bigfoot hunters think they should shoot it. This way they could have **proof**. Other people think this would be bad. They say there are most likely very few Bigfoots. Someone could kill the last one by accident.

No one has found Bigfoot. There are many stories and photos. Most people believe Bigfoot is not real. But that will not stop others from looking.

Some people believe they will see Bigfoot one day.

GLOSSARY

blur
something that is unclear or indistinct

DNA
a type of molecule that makes up all living things

evidence
something that shows something else is true

proof
the facts showing that something is true

track
an imprint left behind from an animal walking on the ground

TRIVIA

1. Some people who fake Bigfoot evidence are trying to make money. They charge money to see prints, fur, and other fake evidence.
2. There are many Bigfoot organizations. They go and look for Bigfoot whenever there is a sighting.
3. The state of Washington has the most Bigfoot reports. As of early 2019, there were more than 650 reports of Bigfoot sightings or other evidence.

ACTIVITY

IMAGINE YOU ARE BIGFOOT

Take a hike with a parent or guardian. Do you see any animal tracks? Can you spot any animals? Imagine you are Bigfoot. Where would you hide? Would you want people to find you? How would you keep people from finding you? What would you eat? When you get home, draw a picture of your adventures. Draw another picture of Bigfoot according to what you imagined.

FURTHER RESOURCES

Want to find out more about Bigfoot?
Check out these resources:

Animal Planet: Two Kids, a Camera, and a Bigfoot
https://www.animalplanet.com/tv-shows/finding-bigfoot/videos/two-kids-a-camera-and-a-bigfoot

Chambers, Catherine. *Bigfoot*. Autobiographies You Never Thought You'd Read! Chicago: Heinemann Raintree, 2016.

Want to find out more about myths and monsters?
Check out these resources:

Mocomi: Mythical Creatures – Part 2
http://mocomi.com/mythical-creatures-part-2

Noll, Elizabeth. *Ghosts*. Strange . . . But True? Mankato, Minn.: Black Rabbit Books, 2018.

INDEX